OLAUDAH

THE INTERESTING MAN

OLAUDAH

EQUIANO

THE INTERESTING MAN

LUKE WALKER

*There is none other name under heaven
given among men, whereby we must be saved.*
Acts 4:12

WRATH AND GRACE

PUBLISHING

INTRODUCTION

Jesus Christ is the representative head of a new humanity; in Adam all die, in Christ all are made alive. Just as "from one blood" God created all nations of people on earth, so from the blood of the Second Adam he is creating one new people from all nations and ethnicities. Christianity is not *the white man's religion*, it is *every man's* religion. Many wicked men and women in the former centuries of our modern times embraced a cultural form of Christianity, but denied its true power (alas! their spiritual offspring yet live among us). But real Christianity ever flies above the cultures of men, transcends their particulars, embraces their diversities, opposes their sins, and offers people from every tribe the only true explanation of their existence, purpose, and high destiny. All things are tending toward this destiny, the great gathering of the lost children of God to the heavenly Zion.[1] My prayer is that this brief look at Olaudah Equiano will edify us in this direction.

My aim in writing is to drive my readers into a deeper study of the remarkable people and events we handle. I have patterned this biography in such a way as to allow the *Interesting Narrative* to retain much of

[1] "Behold, a great multitude that no one could number, from every nation, from all tribes and peoples and languages, standing before the throne and before the Lamb." (Revelation 7:9).

its, well, *interest*. It is the man himself who speaks in its pages; I offer simply a thumbnail sketch and point you in his direction. I urge my readers to acquire and devour the genuine article for themselves.[1]

Equiano's place of birth was contested in his own day, and has recently become a topic of scholarly debate once again. I have given a brief synopsis of the present controversy along with my own conclusions in an appendix.

I would like to thank my most excellent wife Angel for all of her help on this project, Brady Erickson, Nick Larson, Daniel Stanley, and Omri Miles for editing, Anthony Carter for reading the work ahead of time, and John Moore for doing the same, in addition to designing the cover art. I am grateful to God for the opportunity to give this dear brother's biography. May it be a blessing to many.

Luke Walker
Richfield, MN
January 2017

---

[1] I have used the unabridged Broadview edition, edited by Angelo Costanzo, which preserves the *Narrative* in its original two volume format and includes title pages and appendices of relevant documents and quotations.

Dedicated to
My brother John Moore
and
My son Judah Luke

OLAUDAH EQUIANO
THE INTERESTING MAN

Join me, friends, on a journey into the distant memories of men. Spanning some two and a half centuries into the past, we find ourselves in beautiful country, among a people that appear to be African. Many of them are clothed in a stunningly bright and particularly rich shade of blue. Our new friends are clearly a highly civil and clean people. They live in simple, one-story houses in organized villages. We are certainly in a patriarchal society and upon closer inspection the reader of Scripture will be struck by its close resemblance in many points to the children of Israel. They practice circumcision, extensive washings, and enforce strict punishments upon some of the more severe crimes, such as kidnapping and adultery, the latter of which is treated more strictly than almost any other. Their diet is fairly simple. It is an agricultural society, and both men and women work together in the fields. This cooperation, it is believed, is mirrored on the battlefield, where the sexes war side by side. Their only luxuries appear to be the making of fine perfumes and the smoking of tobacco in pipes that are striking for their extremely long length. "Frequently out of grandeur"[1] the pipes of the gentlemen were so long that two young lads

---

[1] Olaudah Equiano, *The Interesting Narrative of the Life of Olaudah Equiano* (Peterborough: Broadview Literary Texts, 2004), 49.

were required to carry them. This was their favorite and chief luxury, so that a man of honor was normally buried along with his favorite pipes.[1]

In the realm of *beliefs*, one doctrinal peculiarity sticks out to us: they are strict predestinarians. They believe that what is ordained to happen will come to pass. The children born here are named after striking events that occur at their birth, or, some presentiment of their future. One such boy was born around the year 1745 and was named Olaudah, which means *fortunate* or *favored*, and it also signifies *having a loud voice* and *being well-spoken*. How fortunate his fate, and how loud and well-spoken his voice, you will have to judge for yourself.

These are the Igbo people of what is modern day Nigeria, in West Africa. These particulars are largely found in a book called *The Interesting Narrative of the Life of Olaudah Equiano*, which was published in the year 1789 in London. The book sparked an entire genre of its own: *the slave narrative*.[2] This style of writing was subsequently taken up by abolitionists and used powerfully to take down the Trans-Atlantic Slave Trade and the wicked institution of slavery it had established.

---

[1] It is also their belief, according to some, that God smokes a pipe.

[2] "It is universally accepted as the fundamental text in the genre of the slave narrative." Vincent Carretta, *Equiano, the African: Biography of a Self-Made Man* (New York: Penguin Books, 2006), xii.

The Interesting Narrative was not the first slave narrative ever to be written, but it was the first *spiritual* slave narrative. Equiano structured it after the *Confessions* of the North African theologian Augustine, which consisted of three parts: first, *slavery and bondage*; secondly, *freedom*, or *salvation*; and thirdly, *the subsequent life*. We will follow this pattern ourselves.

HIS SLAVERY

We find ourselves back in the interior regions of West Africa, where Igbo men and women are working outside of a small village. But where are the children? As usual, they are gathered together in one of the homes, where they go as their parents are away. If trouble comes, the bigger kids will team up and defend the little ones. But, on this very unfortunate day (or, fortunate, it may be, before the end), two of the village children are missing from the group. Olaudah Equiano, 11, is alone with his little sister in their own backyard when, in the blink of an eye, two men and one woman climb over the wall and snatch them both away.

Young boys and girls, when at their homes at play,
Are also caught, and kidnapp'd far away.[1]

Strong hands laid hold of them and they
vanished into the woods. The next day they hit a
main path which Equiano thought he recognized. He
saw people walking up ahead and began to shout.
Would they be delivered so soon? He dared to hope,
and began to taste the forsakenness of false hope
when his captors hushed him up and kept moving.
That night he and his sister cried themselves to sleep
in each other's arms, not knowing what ill fortunes
might await them. Would they ever see their family
again? It wasn't until the next day that *fortune*, that
rough word for God's providence, taught them what
heartbreak really was. They were torn from each
other's arms and his little sister was sold off. Equiano
lost all drive for life. "I was left in a state of dis-
traction not to be described."[2] Who can imagine it?
He refused food, but his captors force-fed him—for
what is dead stock to traders in human flesh and
blood? It is well said to them, "You have lived on
broken hearts all your life."[3]

For several months, he passed in rapid suc-
cession through many different masters, some kinder

[1] Joshua Peel, "On the African Slave-Trade," quoted in Carretta, *Equiano*, 16.
[2] *Interesting Narrative*, 63.
[3] C.S. Lewis, *The Voyage of the "Dawn Treader": Book 3 in The Chronicles of Narnia* (New York: Collier Books, 1970), 50.

than others (but all of them alike owners of human beings). "The African domestic slavery he shows us was quite benign, but it was still slavery—one's own life could change unexpectedly at the whim of another."[1] A relatively kind man purchased him, and *wonder of wonders*, what should he find in the house but his own dear sister! It is to be doubted that he ever tasted such sweet happiness in all his young life. "And thus for a while we forgot our misfortunes in the joy of being together."[2] Here perhaps he would live out his days, a captive, but yoked with his own dear sibling. He banked upon the kindness of this master, but he soon began to learn the truth of that Scripture which says, "Cursed is the man who trusts in man."[3] Alas! How often were his hopes to be dashed upon the rock-hard hearts of men! It was a hard-won lesson he learned throughout his life. "Even this small comfort was soon to have an end."[4] Out of nowhere, his sister was taken from him and sold. This precious little girl here exits the stage; on her future we are entirely in the dark. God knows. "The small relief which her presence gave me from pain was gone, and the wretchedness of my situation was redoubled by my anxiety about her fate."[5] His

---

[1] Carretta, *Equiano*, 26.
[2] *Interesting Narrative*, 66.
[3] Jeremiah 17:5.
[4] *Interesting Narrative*, 66.
[5] Ibid.

anxiety was much to be increased by all that his young eyes were about to see.

He soon found himself among strange men. The closer he approached the sea, the more barbaric were the practices of the people.[1] Shortly his eyes were greeted by the Atlantic Ocean, and a gigantic ship in harbor. "These filled me with astonishment, which was soon converted to terror when I was carried on board."[2] He was told that he would be sold to these even stranger men with white skin. They seemed to be advanced in wickedness, even beyond the more brutal African peoples by the coast. "The white people looked and acted, as I thought, in so savage a manner; for I had never seen among any people such instances of brutal cruelty."[3] He wondered if they were not demons masquerading as men. "I was now persuaded that I had gotten into a world of bad spirits, and that they were going to kill me."[4] Aboard the imposing vessel, he saw one of the crew, a white man, whipped to death with a shipping rope and tossed overboard.

Equiano was soon taken under the deck, where image-bearing human beings were transported to the West Indies to be sold as stock. Here they were

---

[1] "where white men have taught them to be otherwise" John Wesley, *Thoughts Upon Slavery*, Works, vol. 11 (Grand Rapids: Baker Book House, 1979), 64.

[2] *Interesting Narrative*, 70.

[3] Ibid., 71.

[4] Ibid., 70.

forced to lay shackled in eighteen-inch-high compartments. Buckets lined the floor, spilling with filth. Stench suffocated the nostrils while metal and wood squeezed the body. Sickness wasted amongst them; infants fell into the waste buckets and were nearly drowned. "The shrieks of the women, and the groans of the dying, rendered the whole a scene of horror almost inconceivable."[1] What hellish creature devised such cruelty? *Man.* Of course, we're talking about the Middle Passage, where millions of human beings were shipped as cargo from West Africa to the Caribbean. It was now that young Equiano "wished for the last friend, death."[2]

Eventually they made land on the island of Barbados. The slaves were herded like animals, but, ironically, the *civilized* people who swarmed the marketplace more closely resembled the animal kingdom. Families were ripped apart without any regard for the dearest relations in the midst of a wild market. "It was not uncommon to see negroes taken from their wives, wives taken from their husbands, and children from their parents, and sent off to other islands, and wherever else their merciless lords chose; and probably never more during life to see each other!"[3] They were sold without hesitation. "I

---

[1] Ibid., 73.
[2] Ibid., 71.
[3] Ibid., 126.

have been a witness to children torn from their agonized parents."[1] These are the first sufferings of what is known in history books as the Trans-Atlantic Slave Trade.

He spent a few days in Barbados before he was shipped to the United States. In Virginia, an estate owner purchased him and, alas, the child was now separated from the last remnants of his own countrymen. He was brought into the house to stand by the owner's bedside and fan him. In the kitchen, he saw a woman preparing food, weighed down with horrible iron contraptions. The chief of these was known as *the iron muzzle*, which was put on her head and kept her mouth so tightly shut that she wouldn't dare to eat any of the food that she was preparing for her human owners. Passing into the bedroom, he saw things that he couldn't account for. Here he was, in a different world; he took it for magic. A strange contraption went on ticking all by itself, and the eyes of that picture across the room seemed to follow him wherever he went. Was this some form of secret art which allowed these people to preserve their ancestors? He longed for his master to awaken and send him out of the room.

But that ancient will that moves all things was soon kind to Equiano. In his own words, "the kind

---

[1] Olaudah Equiano, *The Interesting Narrative and Other Writings* (New York: Penguin Books, 2003), 334.

and unknown hand of the Creator (who in very deed leads the blind in a way they know not) now began to appear, to my comfort."[1] He was not only dismissed from the magic room, but from this uncaring owner entirely. A gentleman by the name of Michael Henri Pascal, a lieutenant in the British Navy, visited the estate, took a liking to Equiano, and bought him. He followed his new owner onto the ship and they put America behind them. "Every body on board used me very kindly, quite contrary to what I had seen of any white people before; I therefore began to think that they were not all of the same disposition."[2] This was a relative kindness, for some of the people on board told Equiano that they were taking him back to his own country. What! The joy! Of course, it was a cruel trick of heartless men. A much different fate awaited him.

On the voyage to England (for that is where they were really headed), Lieutenant Pascal changed Equiano's name to Gustavus Vassa, the name by which he was known for most of his life. It wasn't until he penned his autobiography that his birth name, Olaudah Equiano, was known again. His namesake, Gustavus Vassa, was a Swedish freedom fighter. It would seem that his second name, like that

---

[1] *Interesting Narrative*, 78.
[2] Ibid., 79.

which he was given at birth, was also filled with presentiments of a noble destiny.

One morning Equiano found the deck of the ship covered with strange white fluff. The crew was eventually able to settle him down and make him understand that it was called *snow*, and that it fell from the sky. He also noticed around this time that his master and his friends were reading books, though he knew not what they were. He wondered how they worked, and wanted greatly to understand them. When he was alone he talked to them and put his ear to them, but, to his alarm, the books never answered him. In time he was to discover how very vocal and well-spoken books were capable of becoming.

Now, my dear reader, consider something with me. Even when we grow up under parental guidance, we are confused about many things. Imagine being a child *alone*, socially isolated with no explanations given while horrors are carried out all around you. That is perhaps the most frightening aspect of all, the psychological terror of the ice-hearted cruelty of men. His first encounters with books and snow, while they may sound funny from the safety of our armchairs, were to him so many occasions of fresh terror. "People generally mock the fears of others when they are themselves in safety."[1]

Equiano served with Lieut. Pascal in the Royal Navy. He saw battle in the Seven Years' War, engaging French vessels at sea and laying siege on land. "During the siege I have counted above sixty shells and carcasses in the air at once."[2] He knew what it was to run back and forth with gunpowder underneath the deck as cannonballs blasted through the walls all around him. "I was a witness of the dreadful fate of many of my companions, who, in the twinkling of an eye, were dashed in pieces, and launched into eternity."[3] He himself expected death at every moment, but he resolved his fears with simple trust in God's sovereignty. "Cheering myself with the reflection that there was a time allotted for me to die as well as to be born, I instantly cast off all fear or thought whatever of death, and went through the whole of my duty with alacrity."[4] His young eyes saw God's hand everywhere, though he knew him not: "Every extraordinary escape, or signal deliverance, either of myself or others, I looked upon to be effected by the interposition of Providence."[5] Thus

---

[1] Ibid., 101.
[2] Ibid., 105.
[3] Ibid., 98-99.
[4] Ibid., 99.
[5] Ibid., 101.

the predestinarian youth fought valiantly, as those who hold this doctrine ever do.[1]

They also sailed to the Mediterranean, to Gibraltar. He was experiencing much of the world; but another world was beginning to open up before him. He was curious about this new religion, and a blessed gentleman by the name of Daniel Queen took Equiano under his wing. "Fortunately this man soon became very much attached to me, and took very great pains to instruct me in many things."[2] Queen began to teach him the Scriptures. As he learned about the children of Israel, his interest was piqued, remembering the customs of his homeland, now so far behind him. He was struck by the similarities. "I was wonderfully surprised to see the laws and rules of my country written almost exactly there."[3] He was thus drawn to the Scriptures. Previously, he had been baptized as a matter of course, but now he began to desire salvation. As yet, however, the mysterious motions of *regeneration* had not been worked upon his heart.

After serving in the war he began to set his sights on freedom. His master's kindness had encouraged

---

[1] The pages of history demonstrate this even in those who have held to fatalism, such as Attila the Hun and Napoleon. "Fatalism has begotten a race of Titans." Loraine Boettner, *The Reformed Doctrine of Predestination* (Phillipsburg: Presbyterian and Reformed Publishing Company), 259.

[2] *Interesting Narrative*, 107.

[3] Ibid.

such hopes. He had also overheard a lawyer tell
Pascal that once he had been baptized, and had
served in the Navy (Pascal had kept all his wages), his
freedom was his due—a prior case had established
precedence in this matter.[1] "I had never once supposed, in all my dreams of freedom, that he would
think of detaining me any longer than I wished."[2] But
the lesson not to trust in men was not as yet grasped
by Equiano in its fullness.

> Fool that I was, inur'd so long to pain,
> To trust to hope, or dream of joy again.[3]

Before he even had a chance to propose the
matter, Pascal turned on him. He brandished a short
sword and threatened to slit his throat if he ran. "I
began, however, to collect myself; and, plucking up
courage, I told him I was free, and he could not by
law serve me so."[4] Like so many unlawful acts that
are committed daily under high heaven, Pascal sold
Equiano to another captain. Just when sweet freedom seemed to present itself, he was thrown into a
cruel time loop and brought back to the West Indies.
As his friends faded out of sight, he says, "I threw
myself on the deck, while my heart was ready to burst

---

[1] See Carretta, *Equiano*, 86-88.
[2] *Interesting Narrative*, 108.
[3] "The Dying Negro," quoted in Carretta, *Equiano*, 113.
[4] *Interesting Narrative*, 108.

with sorrow and anguish."[1] Yet once again he reposed himself on God's sovereignty: "I soon perceived what fate had decreed no mortal on earth could prevent."[2] He greeted his fate, like Gandalf, with a resolved *so be it*.

They arrived on the island of Monserrat. "At the sight of this land of bondage, a fresh horror ran through all my frame, and chilled me to the heart."[3] Upon landing, his misfortunes began immediately: "To comfort me in my distress in that time, two of the sailors robbed me of all my money."[4] Here he was sold to a man named Robert King, a Quaker. To the shame of many contemporary Reformed Christians, the Quakers were highly active in the abolition movement. Many of them were true *friends* to the oppressed. King, not an abolitionist by any stretch of the mind, was relatively kind to Equiano. He didn't beat his slaves, as was custom in the West Indies. If his slaves rose up against him he simply sold them (to masters who would beat them). Thus, the kindest masters in this day were, by comparison to our modern times, unfeeling men. Yet Equiano speaks highly of him: "he possessed a most amiable disposition and temper, and was very charitable and humane."[5]

---

[1] Ibid., 110.
[2] Ibid., 114.
[3] Ibid., 115.
[4] Ibid.
[5] Ibid., 116.

Other *gentlemen* on the island "used to find fault with my master for feeding his slaves so well as he did; although I often went hungry, and an Englishman might think my fare very indifferent."[1]

Equiano served King on trading ships back and forth to Georgia and Philadelphia. He sailed with Captain Thomas Farmer, who was to become his greatest human defendant. He tested Equiano, to see if he would run away, but Equiano's integrity won the day. He believed that if God wanted him to be free, he would find his freedom in the way of open obedience rather than in cunning. "As I was from early years a predestinarian, I thought whatever fate had determined must ever come to pass; and therefore, if ever it were my lot to be freed, nothing could prevent me."[2] This honest integrity did not go unnoticed, nor did it fail in a sort of self-fulfillment. False charges were brought against him and King threatened to sell him, but the captain assured him of their falsehood, and that he had found the young man to be thoroughly trustworthy and upright.

His sincerity was swiftly honored. King encouraged him to save money to buy his freedom. "And, when that was the case, I might depend upon it he would let me have it for forty pounds sterling

---

[1] Ibid., 120.
[2] Ibid., 135.

money."[1] King fronted him sugar and rum, which he traded on the side and kept the profits. Equiano the entrepreneur suffered injustices innumerable, to which he had no legal recourse. If he sold on a white man's word, and that word was not honored, he ate his losses. Slaves had no rights. But by and by he was able to save money.

Before we leave this scene—for leave it we must—let us dwell briefly upon the horrors that Equiano saw in the West Indies. He says were he to list them all, "the catalogue would be tedious and disgusting."[2] Indeed, "every part of the world I had hitherto been in seemed to me a paradise in comparison of the West Indies."[3] There seemed to be something in the air itself that turned otherwise decent men cruel, as if the greed which ran so high in the blood of men was almost contagious. We have glimpsed the horrors of the ships: the shackles, the suffocation, the throwing overboard of the sick and the weak. We've seen the iron muzzle. Time would fail to speak of every cruelty, but we shall not remain silent. Every time a woman was sold in the Caribbean she was violated, on principle. Even the clerks of the relatively mild man, Robert King, religiously observed the perverted custom. "I have even known

[1] Ibid., 141.
[2] Ibid., 129.
[3] Ibid., 135.

[the sailors] to gratify their brutal passion with females not ten years old… as if it were no crime in the whites to rob an innocent African girl of her virtue."[1] What could he do? He was undoubtedly tormented by inescapable thoughts of his little sister, lost so long ago to the raging passions of this demonic system. Unspeakable evil! The living God will yet call it into judgment.

Slaves were beaten for any disobedience. "Indeed on the most trifling occasions they were loaded with chains; and often instruments of torture were added. The iron muzzle, the thumb-screws, &c. are so well known, as not to need a description, and were sometimes applied for the slightest faults."[2] I will not let the reader forget that these were real people, created *imago dei*. "I have seen a negro beaten till some of his bones were broken, for only letting a pot boil over."[3] Ten-to-one, the man who beat him *professed* to be a Christian. Equiano had even heard of such atrocities as a master cutting off a slave's leg for running away. Equiano asked "how he, being a professing Christian, could answer for the horrid act before God. And he told me, answering was a thing of another world; but what he thought and did were

---

[1] Ibid., 120.
[2] Ibid., 123.
[3] Ibid.

policy."[1] Dead religion! "The name of God is blasphemed among the Gentiles because of you."[2]

HIS FREEDOM

Equiano rode many waves of setback and plenty in his toils, but at long last, Equiano the entrepreneur was able to save forty blessed pounds sterling. He met his mark in the city of Savannah, Georgia, where he also "laid out above eight pounds of my money for a suit of superfine clothes to dance in at my freedom, which I hoped was then at hand."[3] They soon arrived in Monserrat, and, "finding myself master of about forty-seven pounds,"[4] he prepared to approach Robert King. His friend, the captain, suggested he come on a certain morning, when he would be there as well. The morning came and he put the named price on the table before King. And, alas! his *friend* the Quaker began to play the quack. King thought what a pity it would be to merely break even on his investment.[5] He was shocked that Equiano could earn such a sum in so short a time,

---

[1] Ibid., 121.

[2] Romans 2:24.

[3] Ibid., 154.

[4] Ibid., 155

[5] This is to say nothing of the years of free income Equiano had earned him, or saved him as a result of his shrewd and diligent work. King estimates the amount *saved* him by Equiano at 100 pounds a year.

and perhaps feigned to disbelieve it. The Fortunate
One was pulverized, his every last hope now dim-
inished to a zero sum. It was all a sham, the sweet
promise of the kindest master he had ever known.
But, glory to God, his friend the captain was there.
"'Come, come,' said my worthy Captain, clapping my
master on the back, 'Come, Robert, (which was his
name) I think you must let him have his freedom.'"[1]
King said he could do him no worse than his word,
and took the hard-earned money for the much-
sought freedom. It was God's will, who could resist?

The once kidnapped child was now a free man!
"My true and worthy friend, the Captain, con-
gratulated us both with a peculiar degree of heart-felt
pleasure."[2] He was given the papers and went
straight to the government building. "My imagination was all rapture…I could scarcely believe I
was awake… All within my breast was tumult,
wildness, and delirium! My feet scarcely touched the
ground, for they were winged with joy."[3] The party
was arranged, and the long-awaited night arrived on
which he was to dance his freedom. "At the dances
I gave, my Georgia superfine blue clothes made no
indifferent appearance, as I thought. Some of the
sable females, who formerly stood aloof, now began

---

[1] *Interesting Narrative*, 155.

[2] Ibid., 156.

[3] Ibid.

to relax and appear less coy."[1] Yes, the interesting man was growing in interest and stature. Outfit *on fleek*, the princely character grew.

He worked for Robert King as a hired freeman, earning wages on his ships. His kind friend, the captain, died a few months after he had gained his freedom. He called Equiano to his deathbed and "asked (with almost his last breath) if he had ever done me any harm? 'God forbid I should think so,' I replied, 'I should then be the most ungrateful of wretches to the best of benefactors.'"[2] He expired as Equiano spoke. "I found that I did not know, till he was gone, the strength of my regard for him."[3] Oh, how he blessed God for that warm friend in a cold world! "Had it pleased Providence that he had died but five months before, I verily believe I should not have obtained my freedom when I did; and it is not improbable that I might not have been able to get it at any rate afterwards."[4]

It just so happened that the captain died while they were out at sea, leaving no one on board to take over. Equiano himself took the helm and brought the ship back to Robert King—nearly a ten-day journey, and no small feat for one untrained in navigation. "Many were surprised when they

[1] Ibid., 158.
[2] Ibid., 163.
[3] Ibid.
[4] Ibid.

heard…and I now obtained a new appellation, and was called Captain…as high a title as any free man in this place possessed."[1] This no doubt tickled his fancy, as he says of himself at this hour, "The sable captain lost no fame."[2] There were more adventures for *the captain*, but I shall send my readers to the *Interesting Narrative* for those.

He longed above all else to return to England, "where my heart had always been,"[3] and see his old friends. He bid farewell to Robert King and happily quitted the West Indies. In London, he ran into Pascal, who asked how he had come back. "I answered, 'In a ship.' To which he replied dryly, 'I suppose you did not walk back to London on the water.'"[4] His return from the West Indies was undeniably a miraculous appearance, a sort of resurrection from the dead.

In London, he trained as a barber (or, as he puts it, a *hairdresser*), and mastered the French horn, in addition to studying mathematics and learning the art of making salt water fresh under Dr. Charles Irving ("reducing old Neptune's dominions," as he has it).[5] Not yet a landlubber, he hired himself out to rich men on board commercial and Navy ships. He

---

[1] Ibid., 164.
[2] Ibid.
[3] Ibid., 165.
[4] Ibid., 181.
[5] Ibid., 189.

travelled to Smyrna and to Portugal, where he was greeted with the dying efforts of our old foe the Roman Catholic Church. "None of us even dared to go on board any other vessel or on shore till the Inquisition had sent on board and searched for every thing illegal, especially bibles...and any person in whose custody a bible was found concealed was to be imprisoned and flogged, and sent into slavery for ten years."[1] Such were the abolitionist efforts of Rome. He was curious of their conjurings and entered their gates with the necessary sprinkling of holy water. "From curiosity, and a desire to be holy, I therefore complied with this ceremony, but its virtues were lost on me, for I found myself nothing the better for it."[2]

Back in England, an explorer by the name of Constantine John Phipps was hatching plots to strike a northern passage to India, and Equiano attended Dr. Irving on this voyage. Thus they journeyed north, if not in hopes of fortune, certainly in hopes of fame. Equiano almost died several times on this voyage. While writing at night in his journal, a spark from his candle caught on some of the combustibles in the storeroom around him. "Immediately the whole was in a blaze. I saw nothing but present death before me, and expected to be the first to perish in

---

[1] Ibid., 185.
[2] Ibid.

the flames."[1] But the crew rushed with blankets to put out the inferno. Fire now being defeated, frost lay ahead as his next foe. Equiano fell into the arctic waters and was nearly drowned; his body would have been preserved, perhaps, until the end of time. Yet it would have been to a resurrection of judgment, for he was not yet ready for the greatest journey of all, *death*. In his own words:

> Our deplorable condition, which kept up the constant apprehensions of our perishing in the ice, brought me gradually to think of eternity in such a manner as I never had done before. I had the fears of death hourly upon me, and shuddered at the thoughts of meeting the grim king of terrors in the *natural* state I was then in, and was exceedingly doubtful of a happy eternity if I should die in it.[2]

Before the northern journey Equiano professed to be a Christian, thinking he was a righteous man. But as death moved in on him he was awakened to the truth that he was not ready to stand before his Maker. His life being spared, eternity was pressed

---

[1] Ibid., 190.
[2] Ibid., 192.

upon him. Turned back by the ice, they returned safely to England, and there he wrestled with God:

> I began seriously to reflect on the dangers I had escaped…which made a lasting impression on my mind, and, by the grace of God, proved afterwards a mercy to me; it caused me to reflect deeply on my eternal estate, and to seek the Lord with full purpose of heart ere it was too late… I became a burden to myself, and viewed all things around me as emptiness and vanity, which could give no satisfaction to a troubled conscience… I was under strong convictions of sin, and thought that my state was worse than any man's…I often wished for death, though at the same time convinced I was altogether unprepared for that awful summons… [God] was pleased, in much mercy, to give me to see, and in some measure to understand, the great and awful scene of the judgment-day, that "no unclean person, no unholy thing, can enter into the kingdom of God."[1]

He was "determined…to be a first-rate Christian."[2] He knew not where to turn, and found no life

[1] Ibid., 197.
[2] Ibid., 194.

in visiting churches. He determined to read the
gospels, and sought to find a sect or society that lived
in accordance with them. After looking near and
far—in London!—not even one was found. He visited the Quaker meetings, and "remained as much in
the dark as ever;" he studied the Roman Catholic
Church, but "was not in the least edified;" and he
even explored Judaism.[1] But alas, the one question
that is ever pressed upon the convicted sinner's con-
science found no answer in all these. "I knew not
where to seek shelter from the wrath to come."[2]
Utterly distraught, he resolved to return to the Middle East because he "really thought the Turks were
in a safer way of salvation than my neighbours."[3]
Finally, repulsed by the dead religion all around him,
he "resolved, at that time, never more to return to
England."[4]

Prevented from going to Turkey by the Arm that
moves all things, he began to beg the Lord to change
his heart. "I appealed to the Searcher of hearts,
whether I did not wish to love him more, and serve
him better. Notwithstanding all this, the reader may
easily discern, if he is a believer, that I was still in
nature's darkness."[5] He begged for space to repent,

---

[1] Ibid., 194-95.
[2] Ibid., 164.
[3] Ibid., 195.
[4] Ibid., 197.
[5] Ibid., 198.

and to be lead into godly company, where he might be guided. He fell into company with "an old sea-faring man, who experienced much of the love of God shed abroad in his heart."[1] Equiano "had never heard before the love of Christ to believers set forth in such a manner, and in so clear a point of view."[2] A minister entered the house and asked him where he heard the gospel preached. "I knew not what he meant by hearing the gospel."[3] He was then invited to a love-feast in their chapel that evening. It was unlike anything he had ever seen, except that he had read about it in the Scriptures. He finally discovered a people that walked with the God of the Bible. "Much was said by every speaker of the providence of God, and his unspeakable mercies, to each of them."[4] Of this he knew much, "but when they spoke of a future state, they seemed to be altogether certain of their calling and election of God; and that no one could ever separate them from the love of Christ, or pluck them out of his hands."[5] He was shocked:

> This filled me with utter consternation, intermingled with admiration. I was so

---

[1] Ibid.
[2] Ibid., 199
[3] Ibid., 198.
[4] Ibid., 199.
[5] Ibid., 200.

amazed as not to know what to think of the company; my heart was attracted and my affections were enlarged. I wished to be as happy as them, and was persuaded in my mind that they were different from the world "that lieth in wickedness" I John v. 19... I was entirely overcome, and wished to live and die thus... This kind of Christian fellowship I had never seen, nor ever thought of seeing on earth; it fully reminded me of what I had read in the holy scriptures, of the primitive Christians, who loved each other and broke bread... I saw that time was very short, eternity long, and very near, and I viewed those persons alone blessed who were found ready at midnight call, or when the Judge of all both quick and dead, cometh." ... I was soon connected with those whom the scripture calls the excellent of the earth. I heard the gospel preached, and the thoughts of my heart and actions were laid open by the preachers, and the way of salvation by Christ alone was evidently set forth. [1]

---

[1] Ibid 200-01.

Thus he began to ask, to seek, and to knock at that blessed and fearful gate of salvation. "I resolved to win Heaven if possible; and if I perished I thought it should be at the feet of Jesus, in praying to him for salvation."[1] He heard of a man dying in full assurance of salvation and marveled greatly. "Confusion, anger, and discontent seized me, and I staggered much at this sort of doctrine; it brought me to a stand, not knowing which to believe, whether salvation by works or by faith only in Christ."[2] His new friends exhorted him, and he began to wrestle with the question of the ages—the question that awakened old Master Wycliffe, and tormented the Augustinian monk of Germany—that question which is destined to awaken all nations of men: *is salvation by works or by faith?* A minister at this time "assured me, that one sin unatoned for was as sufficient to damn a soul as one leak was to sink a ship. Here I was struck with awe; for the minister exhorted me much, and reminded me of the shortness of time, and the length of eternity, and that no unregenerate soul, or any thing unclean, could enter the kingdom of Heaven."[3]

He returned to sea, hiring himself on a ship named Hope. "I wrestled hard with God in fervent prayer, who had declared in his word that he would

[1] Ibid., 200.
[2] Ibid., 202.
[3] Ibid., 203-04.

hear the groanings and deep sighs of the poor in spirit. I found this verified to my astonishment in the following manner."[1] On the morning of October 6, 1774, he awoke with the sense that something remarkable was going to happen that day. As he read the Scriptures, he came to Acts chapter four, and the twelfth verse seemed to jump off the page: "There is no other name under heaven by which men must be saved." As he meditated upon these words, astonishing things began to happen. But we shall hear it from the man himself:

> I began to think I had lived a moral life…not knowing whether salvation was to be had partly for our own good deeds, or solely as the sovereign gift of God; in this deep consternation the Lord was pleased to break in upon my soul with his bright beams of heavenly light; and in an instant as it were, removing the veil, and letting light into a dark place. I saw clearly with the eye of faith the crucified Savior, bleeding on the cross on Mount Calvary: the scriptures became an unsealed book, I saw myself a condemned criminal under the law, which came with its full force to my conscience… I saw the Lord

---

[1] Ibid., 205.

Jesus Christ in his humiliation, loaded and bearing my reproach, sin, and shame. I then clearly perceived that by the deeds of the law no flesh living could be justified…. It was given to me at that time to know what it is to be born again… The word of God was sweet to my taste, yea sweeter than honey and the honeycomb. Christ was revealed to my soul as the chiefest among ten thousand. These heavenly moments were really as life to the dead… Now every leading providential circumstance that happened to me, from the day I was taken from my parents to that hour, was then in my view, as if it had but just then occurred. I was sensible of the invisible hand of God which guided and protected me when in truth I knew it not: still the Lord pursued me… The amazing things of that hour can never be told.[1]

He left his room and tried to tell his shipmates what was transpiring. "I became a barbarian to them in talking of the love of Christ."[2] They had no idea the things of which his ecstatic soul spoke. "His name was to me as ointment poured forth. Now the Bible was my only companion and comfort. When-

[1] Ibid., 205-06.
[2] Ibid., 207.

ever I looked in the Bible I saw new things."[1] He was regenerated, he was washed, he was justified, on that blessed day. "By free grace I was persuaded that I had a part in the first resurrection... I wished for a man of God with whom I might converse: my soul was like the chariots of Aminidab, Canticles vi. 12."[2]

> He dy'd for all who ever saw
> No help in them, nor by the law: –
> I this have seen; and gladly own
> "Salvation is by Christ alone!"[3]

He longed to see the lost converted, to return to London and tell his friends the great news, and yet he longed more than even these things to be with the Lord Jesus Christ. "Now my whole wish was to be dissolved and to be with Christ! But alas, I must wait mine appointed time."[4] Much was to be accomplished before that blessed hour came. All was being arranged; he must yet fulfill his destiny and send his well-spoken voice across nations.

---

[1] Ibid.
[2] Ibid.
[3] Ibid., 213.
[4] Ibid., 209.

HIS SUBSEQUENT LIFE

With what joy did his friends in London greet the news! It was clear that *the African* was now an heir of heaven. The believers around him encouraged him to serve God with the seafaring gifts he had. His zeal for seeing others taste the grace of God grew, and he was frequently the godliest character on board. We might say the sable captain had become the sable *chaplain.*[1] In Spain, a priest tried to convert him to Roman Catholicism, and went so far as to tell him he might become pope one day. "On these occasions I used to produce my Bible, and shew him in what points his church erred."[2] The priest offered him a free education in the Catholic universities, but Equiano refused. "I was therefore enabled to regard the word of God, which says, 'Come out from amongst them,' and refused Father Vincent's offer... so we parted without conviction on either side."[3] A Protestant without guile!

He was soon invited by Dr. Irving to oversee his new plantation at the Musquito Shore of Central America—undoubtedly a matter of confliction for Equiano. But, by the good advice of his friends, with an eye to the ready harvest in that part of the world,

---

[1] He had also previously performed a burial service. See ibid., 177.

[2] Ibid., 216.

[3] Ibid.

he obliged, hoping "to be the instrument, under God, of bringing some poor sinner to my well beloved master, Jesus Christ."[1] He met a group of Musquito natives with Dr. Irving, who had been ill used in England and were about to travel home to Central America on Her Majesty's dollar.[2] "I was very much mortified in finding that they had not frequented any churches since they were here, to be baptized, nor was any attention paid to their morals. I was very sorry for this mock Christianity, and had just an opportunity to take some of them once to church before we sailed."[3]

He sailed with these natives and "took all the pains that I could to instruct the Indian prince in the doctrines of Christianity…and, to my great joy, he was quite attentive, and received with gladness the truths that the Lord enabled me to set forth… I had Fox's Martyrology…and he used to be very fond of looking into it, and would ask many questions about the papal cruelties he saw depicted there, which I explained to him."[4] However, mocked by his countrymen, the young prince rejected the gospel and isolated himself for the remainder of the trip. May it be that he came to faith later on, and that we

---

[1] Ibid., 218.
[2] *Pound*, rather.
[3] *Interesting Narrative.*, 219.
[4] Ibid.

may find ourselves feasting with him in the kingdom of God!

His mild work as an overseer in Central America completed, Equiano hired himself on a boat back to England—not, of course, without narrowly escaping a kidnapping back into slavery. When he returned to London he was burdened exceedingly to work for the cause of abolition. He joined the Sierra Leone Project, a government-funded effort to resettle former slaves in West Africa. He desired to see Africa affected by the gospel, *reformed*, and prospered by vibrant participation in Trans-Atlantic free trade.[1] Equiano the capitalist "envisioned a black colonial government, the replacement of the slave trade by 'legitimate trade,' and the entry of ordinary African people into the Atlantic market as producers and consumers."[2]

He discovered misappropriation of funds within the Sierra Leone Project and was fired for seeking to expose the corruption. He then founded, with other former slaves like himself, *The Sons of Africa*, a group which fought for the rights of Afro-Britains. *The Society for Effecting the Abolition of the Slave Trade* was working at this time as well; Granville Sharp sat as its

---

[1] Early abolitionists utilized the economics of Adam Smith, himself anti-slavery, against their pro-slavery opponents.
[2] John Saillant, *Black Puritan, Black Republican: The Life and Thought of Lemuel Haynes* (New York: Oxford University Press, 2003), 149.

chair.[1] The likes of William Wilberforce and Thomas Clarkson labored with *the Society*. They also worked with former slave-trader turned hymn-writer John Newton, who brought forward his painful eye-witness testimonies in the cause.

It was now that Equiano was encouraged to put his life on paper, and thus he began to pen his *Interesting Narrative*. It is said that he "transformed his entire life into a sort of anti-slavery document,"[2] as he chronicled the "hardships which are inseparable from this accursed trade."[3] He finished it in the year 1789. Wilberforce was to speak before Parliament; Equiano was racing to finish his account to aid in the cause. It was now time for the Loud One to *bring the noise*. "It thrust Equiano into the centre of the national debate on slavery."[4] The first edition had 311 subscribers, including the Prince of Wales, the Duke of York, and fifteen members of Parliament, besides citizens of high standing and ministers.[5] It *sold*. Nine editions were issued in five years.[6] Equiano

[1] Granville Sharp was a prominent evangelical scholar of biblical Greek. In fact, a significant Greek rule, which demonstrates the deity of Christ from 2 Peter 1:1, was proven by Sharp and named after him, *the Granville Sharp construct*.

[2] Brycchan Carey, "Olaudah Equiano: An Illustrated Biography," http://www.brycchancarey.com/equiano/biog.htm.

[3] *Interesting Narrative*, 74.

[4] Ibid., 11.

[5] Subscribers paid some money down and pledged to buy a certain number of copies. The practice was widespread among authors and helped assure sellers of a book's prospective success.

[6] By the ninth edition the number of subscribers had grown to 894.

self-promoted the book; he travelled throughout England and the British Isles, speaking and selling. He was a true entrepreneur, with his hand in every part of the work. In fact, unlike most contemporary authors, Equiano retained sole control over his work rather than selling his rights to a bookseller for a lump sum. He was the definition of a self-made man. Some have called him the black Ben Franklin. But, since his autobiography preceded Franklin's by decades, it is better to think of Franklin as the white Equiano.[1]

Hold onto your tricornes, from here our timeline runs swiftly ahead. In 1791, William Wilberforce brought a motion for abolition in Parliament; it was defeated. In 1792, Olaudah Equiano married Susanna Cullen, a white woman. Upon his first arrival to England he "could not help remarking the particular slenderness of their women, which I did not at first like."[2] Eventually, he went so far as to *love* one of these slender women. He wrote to a friend, "I now mean as it seem Pleasing to my Good God!— to leave London in about 8—or, 10 Days more, & take me a Wife."[3] He became a great advocate for mixed marriages, a sort of free love market to go with

---

[1] "...rather than considering Equiano an African American Franklin we would more accurately call Franklin an Anglo-American Equiano." Carretta, *Equiano*, xiii.

[2] *Interesting Narrative*, 83.

[3] *Interesting Narrative and Other Writings*, 358.

the free trade he envisioned between England and West Africa. He wrote to an opponent, "Away then with your narrow impolitic notion of preventing by law what will be a national honour, national strength, and productive of national virtue—Intermarriages!"[1] This sentiment was shared by early abolitionists. "Indeed, virtually all eighteenth-century commentary on abolition, from both the defenders and the critics of slavery, assumed future interactions of all sorts (commercial, political, religious, sexual) between blacks and whites were they to live in one society."[2]

They had a daughter the next year named Anna Marie, and a second, Joanna, two years later. That same year, 1792, Wilberforce's bill was once again defeated in Parliament. In 1796, just four years after they were married, Susanna Vassa died. And Mr. Olaudah Equiano himself, the Interesting Man of many names, died in the year 1797. His appointed time, that which he had saluted from afar so many years before, had come. He put off his body of death and entered into God's paradise. His little girl Anna Marie died that same year. He was survived only by his youngest daughter Joanna, who was a mere two years old.

The slave trade was finally abolished in England in 1807. Nine years later, Joanna Vassa inherited her

---

[1] Ibid., 332.

[2] Saillant, *Black Puritan, Black Republican*, 6.

father's fortune on her 21st birthday.[1] The Slavery
Abolition Act was passed by Parliament in 1833, in
no small part due to the testimony of our dear friend
the African. In 1845 African American abolitionist
Frederick Douglass penned his famous autobiography, fashioned in the likeness of Equiano's. The
last domino fell in 1863, when President Abraham
Lincoln signed the Emancipation Proclamation. The
fortunate course of these events is in no small measure
the legacy of Olaudah Equiano.

THE REFORMATION AND ABOLITION

One of the great miracles of the gospel is that
many slaves were able to see through the hypocrisy
of their "Christian" masters and embrace the real
Christ. To them, Christianity was not *the white man's
religion*. No, they perceived that these cruel men lived
a mock version of the genuine article. Frederick
Douglass puts it in the strongest terms: "Between the
Christianity of this land, and the Christianity of
Christ, I recognize the widest possible difference —
so wide, that to receive the one as good, pure, and
holy, is of necessity to reject the other as bad,

---

[1] At his death Equiano was the wealthiest person of African descent in the
British Empire.

corrupt, and wicked."[1] Equiano has it: "O, ye nominal Christians! might not an African ask you, learned you this from your God? who says unto you, Do unto all men as you would men should do unto you?"[2] The reality is, Christians deserve the lion's share of the credit for the abolition of race-based slavery in the West.[3]

Unfortunately, some prominent Reformed theologians took their part in the wicked institution described in this book. The name of Jonathan Edwards carries, for many, a tinge of uneasiness. He participated in and even defended the slavery of his own day.[4] George Whitefield—whom Equiano heard preach in person with great joy[5]—did as well.[6] We don't doubt the sincere faith, great zeal, and

---

[1] Frederick Douglass, *The Narrative of the Life of Frederick Douglass* (New York: Dover Publications, 1995), 71.

[2] *Interesting Narrative*, 76.

[3] I do not mean to say that they were all true believers.

[4] "We have precious little regarding Edwards' formal doctrine of slavery... The one time [he] officially addresses slavery, he finds himself defending a slave owner who rejects his theology against a group of parishioners who support his theology." Thabiti Anyabwile, "Jonathan Edwards, Slavery, and the Theology of African Americans,"
https://blogs.thegospelcoalition.org/justintaylor/files/2012/02/Thabiti-Jonathan-Edwards-slavery-and-theological-appropriation.pdf.

[5] "When I got into the church I saw this pious man exhorting the people with the greatest fervour and earnestness, and sweating as much as I ever did while in slavery on Montserrat beach... I had never seen divines exert themselves in this manner before, and I was no longer at a loss to account for the thin congregations they preached to," *Interesting Narrative*, 152-53.

[6] Before relaying his own purchase of a planation and slaves, he says, "The constitution of that colony [Georgia] is very bad, and it is impossible for the inhabitants to subsist without the use of slaves." Quoted by Rev. L. Tyerman *The Life of the Rev. George Whitefield, B.A., of Pembroke College Oxford, Vol. II* (London: Hodder and Stoughton, 1890), 169.

extreme giftedness of an Edwards or a Whitefield;
we fully expect to meet them at table with joy in the
kingdom. We are ashamed, however, of their pos-
ition on this inexcusable atrocity. Equiano, fore-
seeing our modern sentiments, urged the cause of
ethnic equality with an eye to the future: "Actions
like these are the just and sure foundation of future
fame."[1]

Reformed theology itself has a greater story to
tell. As we've seen in Wycliffe, the cause of free men
in free societies is simply the working out of the
principles of the Reformation. Reformed theology
inevitably set itself against this most wicked brand of
slavery. "Equiano attacked the basis of racial slavery
from an ostensibly Protestant worldview."[2] He was a
blue-blooded Calvinist. In fact, it was his Calvinism
that demanded recognition of the dignity of *all
peoples*. As Reformed theology has it, all the children
of Adam are on equal footing, *dead in trespasses and
sins*, and unable to come to God; further, God has
given his Son a people from all tribes and nations. If
the blood of Christ was shed for people from all
nations, then God values all image-bearing ethnicities alike. Others would wax yet warmer. Later in
our studies we will find *the Black Puritan*, Lemuel

---

[1] *Interesting Narrative*, 249.
[2] Eric Washington, "Slaveholder, How Will You Answer God?"
http://thefrontporch.org/2015/04/slaveholder-how-will-you-answer-god.

Haynes, taking up Calvinism and leveling mighty blows against the institution of slavery with the formidable weapon such a theology is.

Equiano was converted under the ministry of Calvinistic Methodists.[1] He saw God's sovereignty as the only explanation for his own experience; the truths of Scripture on this point, as on all points, squared with reality. "For Equiano, there was no other plausible way to think about the outcome of his life."[2] It may be argued that his upbringing as a predestinarian affected his later Calvinism; I don't deny it. But Equiano himself was convinced that the Igbo had sprung from Israel, and had thus received teachings from the Bible in the first place.[3] His conversion to Calvinism was, it seems, a sort of theological coming of age; interestingly, in going from predestinarian to Reformed Calvinist, he fulfilled his destiny. *The African* was *the Black Calvinist*, but he wasn't the only one. Lemuel Haynes, Jupiter Hammon, and Phillis Wheatley are notables in this regard. "Calvinism seems to have corroborated the deepest structuring elements of the experience of such men and women as they matured from children

---

[1] "Though he heard the gospel from a 'Dissenting minister,' who was clearly a Methodist, the tone and tenor of this minister's preaching was clearly Reformed Protestant." Eric Washington, "Calvinism: Inherently Anti-Slavery?" http://thefrontporch.org/2015/04/calvinism-inherently-anti-slavery/.

[2] Ibid.

[3] He cites the likes of Thomas Clarkson and John Gill to this purpose.

living in slavery or servitude into adults desiring freedom, literacy, and membership in a fair society."[1] They believed that God's sovereign purposes alone made real sense of the Afro-British and African American experience.

Reformed theology necessarily mobilized white Christians as well. William Wilberforce gave his life to the cause. John Newton added dreadful testimony of his time on slave ships. The names of William Cowper, Granville Sharp, and the Puritan Richard Baxter can all be found on the roll of abolitionists. John Wesley, not a Calvinist, but a law and gospel preacher, was also an abolitionist. He was one of Equiano's subscribers, and read the *Narrative* on his deathbed. The last letter he ever wrote was to Wilberforce, encouraging him in this good work; it was, as it were, his expiring breath. Our good friend Charles Spurgeon was a hearty abolitionist as well. An American Southern newspaper threatened to lynch him for it: "If the Pharisaical author should ever show himself in these parts, we trust that a stout cord may speedily find its way around his eloquent throat" [2]—we think it had better be a doubly *stout* cord to keep that brother off the ground. And when

---

[1] Saillant, *Black Puritan, Black Republican*, 4.

[2] *The Southern Reporter and Daily Commercial Courier*, April 10, 1860. See Christian George, "The Reason Why America Burned Spurgeon's Sermons and Sought to Kill Him," http://center.spurgeon.org/2016/09/22/the-reason-why-america-burned-spurgeons-sermons-and-sought-to-kill-him.

we look back at a John Calvin, we are happy to find in him these same anti-slavery sentiments. He calls the harsh brand of slavery described in this book as something "which cannot be done according to the manners that are among us."[1] Equiano anticipated the thankfulness we presently feel for such men when he said, "*Then* shall those persons particularly be named with praise and honour, who generously proposed and stood forth in the cause of humanity, liberty, and good policy."[2]

The societal freedoms we enjoy today find their historical headwaters in the Protestant Reformation. The Reformers were the human instruments; the gospel itself did the work. "There is no doubt that Equiano believed that spiritual redemption is the ultimate redemption; but he recognized aspects of social redemption."[3] The gospel of God's free grace for all peoples in Jesus Christ flew into collision with the Trans-Atlantic Slave Trade. "Strange that in a land which boasts of the purest light of the Gospel, and the most perfect freedom, there should be found advocates of oppression—for the most abject and iniquitous kind of slavery."[4] He recognized and celebrated the societal, literary, scientific, and economic

---

[1] *John Calvin's Sermons on 1 Timothy*, Ray Van Neste and Brian Denker, ed. Kindle Edition, Sermon 46 on 1 Timothy 6:1-2.

[2] *Interesting Narrative*, 249. Emphasis mine.

[3] Washington, "Calvinism: Inherently Anti-Slavery?"

[4] *Interesting Narrative and Other Writings*, 332.

advances of England; he pointed to slavery, as if to say, *one thing you lack*. It was Reformed theology in Equiano which called England to repentance.

In the end, we can most assuredly say that the living God knows how to bring good out of much evil. After our brief glance at the Interesting Man, would you say that he was named correctly, *fortunate* and *favored*? Was he *a loud voice*, and *well-spoken*? His book ran through the populace, and he spoke before rulers! His (un)fortunate experiences were not for his good alone; they were for the good of many. He came to bless the day that he was put in the way of the gospel, even by wicked men. And through his sufferings, God spread the gospel to thousands and brought earthly freedom to millions.

Such studies as these are valuable to those with eyes to see. For them, the encouragement is clear: When an inconvenience, or some great suffering, comes your way, embrace it. You never know what interesting plans the living God has up his sleeve. We shall end where Equiano does:

> After all, what makes any event important, unless by its observation we become better and wiser, and learn "to do justly, to love mercy, and to walk humbly before God"? To those who are possessed of this spirit, there is scarcely any book or incident so trifling

that it does not afford some profit, while to others the experience of ages seems of no use; and even to pour out to them the treasures of wisdom is throwing the jewels of instruction away.[1]

THE END.

---

[1] *Interesting Narrative*, 252-53.

APPENDIX
THE QUESTION OF EQUIANO'S BIRTHPLACE

Equiano's claim of Igbo birth was contested in his own lifetime. It was asserted that his true birthplace was the Caribbean island of St. Croix. He responded to these accusations in the 1792 edition of the *Narrative*: "it is only needful of me to appeal to those numerous and respectable persons of character who knew me when I first arrived in England, and could speak no language but that of Africa."[1]

In recent times, fresh controversy has arisen about his place of birth. Vincent Carretta (University of Maryland) has brought forward two pieces of historical evidence which assert a birthplace not of West Africa, but of South Carolina. The documents in question are baptismal records from 1759 and a ship log from 1773, both of which record South Carolina as Equiano's place of birth.

Carretta's findings have sparked new interest in Equiano's narrative and the man behind it. Before voicing my own conclusions, we must ask, does Carretta take Equiano as a fraud? No. Far from diminishing his authority, in Carretta's eyes, these findings have served to raise his esteem of Equiano as a writer. Is it possible that the descriptive flourishes which begin his autobiography were literary

---

[1] *Interesting Narrative*, 255.

devises used to depict, if not his literal experience, what in truth did happen to him as a descendant of kidnapped West Africans? Carretta's conclusion is certainly intriguing: "My Equiano is a literary genius. Other people's Equiano is more like a literary tape recorder: He says what he says."[1] Equiano placed himself squarely in the latter category;[2] it is possible, however, to be *both*.

There are alternative interpretations of the evidence. Paul Lovejoy (York University) contends that matters such as his circumcision (not practiced in either South Carolina or England at the time) and the corroboration of witnesses as to his only speaking an African tongue when he first arrived in England point to a genuine Igbo birth. My own conclusion, in addition to these considerations, is as follows.

The ship records from the Phipps voyage rest on the old baptismal records (a rough form of ID). As a free man facing such threats of injustice and recapture into slavery that he himself testifies of in the *Narrative*, it would be madness for him to dispute his own precious forms of identification. "The proof that he was free depended upon his baptismal identification stating his birth in South Carolina and

---

[1] Quoted by Teresa Wiltz, "For Slave's Biographer, Truth Contains A Bit of Fiction," http://www.washingtonpost.com/wp-dyn/content/article/2005/09/09/AR2005090902079.html.

[2] He calls himself "one who was as unwilling as unable to adorn the plainness of truth by the colouring of imagination." *Interesting Narrative*, 252.

his manumission from Robert King… Vassa was unlikely to have changed his baptismal testimony, whether true or not."[1] The question then seems to come down to the integrity of *the baptismal record* itself.

Equiano was known by those around him to be a deeply sincere disciple of Jesus Christ. Godly names are attached to his legacy. Is it not conceivable that an unregenerate child, only a short time into a trauma of the magnitude described in this book, might be moved, for one reason or another, to falsely testify his place of birth? Is it not possible that the records themselves were logged against knowledge by a hand other than Equiano's? We simply don't know.

In the end, it appears that what we have is the word of Equiano the regenerate man versus the supposed word of Equiano the unregenerate child. I for my part take the endorsements of the godly people who surrounded him as proof of his godly character, which I, in turn, take as proof of his *honesty* when he says he was born in Igboland.[2]

[1] Paul E. Lovejoy, *Olaudah Equiano or Gustavus Vassa: What's in a Name?* Atlantic Studies, Vol. 9, No. 2, June 2012, 171.

[2] Granville Sharp, after visiting him on his deathbed, says, "He was a sober, honest man." Quoted in Carretta, *Equiano*, 366.

95374587R00035

Made in the USA
Columbia, SC
15 May 2018